POINT OF IMPACT

Revised and Updated

Heinemann Library
Chicago, Illinois

Penicillin

A Breakthrough in Medicine

Customer Service 888-454-2279
Visit our website at www.heinemannraintree.com

Designed by Tokay Interactive Ltd. (www.tokay.co.uk)
Printed in China by WKT Ltd

10 09 08 07 06
10 9 8 7 6 5 4 3 2 1

New edition ISBNs:1-40349-141-0 (hardcover)
                  1-40349-150-X (paperback)

The Library of Congress has cataloged the first edition as follows:
Tames, Richard.
      Penicillin : a breakthrough in medicine / Richard Tames.
            p. cm. — (Point of impact)
      Previously published in Great Britain by Heinemann Library.
      Includes bibliographical reference and index.
      Summary: Describes the development of penicillin, from its discovery and use in World War II to the possible implications of overuse.
      ISBN 1-57572-417-0 (library binding)
      1. Penicillin—History—Juvenile literature. [1. Penicillin.] I. Title. II. Series.

RM666.P35 T36 2000
615'.3295654—dc21
                                                        00-026088

Acknowledgments
The publishers would like to thank the following for permission to reproduce photographs: Corbis: (Bettmann) pp. **4**, **17**, **20**, **21**, (Hulton Deutsch Collection) pp. **18**, **19**; Hulton Getty Images: pp. (John Chillingworth) **23**; Mary Evans Picture Library: p. **6**; MIG/Audio Visual Services/ICSM (St. Mary's): pp. **12**, **13**, **14**, **15**, **22**, **24**; Science Photo Library: (Andrew McClenaghan) p. **26**, (Sheila Terry) p. **27**; Tames, Richard: pp. **5**, **8**, **11**, **16**, **25**; Wellcome Institute Library, London: pp. **7**, **9**, **10**.

Cover photograph reproduced with permission of Science Photo Library / SCIMAT.

The publishers would like to thank Stewart Ross for his help in the preparation of this book.

Every effort has been made to contact copyright holders of any material reproduced in this book. Any omissions will be rectified in subsequent printings if notice is given to the publisher.

The paper used to print this book comes from sustainable resources.

Contents

Hoping for a Miracle   4

From Magic to Medicine   6

Defeating Smallpox   8

Science Strengthens Medicine   10

A Life in Science   12

Dissolving in Tears   14

Penicillin   16

A Breakthrough   18

A Problem of Production   20

Into Battle   22

Prizewinners   24

Battling On   26

The Great Debate   28

Find Out More   29

Timeline   30

Glossary   31

Index   32

Some words are shown in bold, **like this**. You can find out what they mean by looking in the Glossary.

Hoping for a Miracle

Race against death

In late summer 1943, two-year-old Patricia Malone lay in New York's Lutheran Hospital with a rare form of blood **infection**. Doctors told her parents she would die within seven hours. Patricia's father had heard of a new wonder drug called penicillin, which was only being given to soldiers. He called a journalist friend, begging him to help get some for Patricia.

The journalist called the surgeon general in Washington, D.C. The surgeon general called Dr. Chester Keefer in Boston. Keefer was in charge of the penicillin production project. He ordered a laboratory in New Brunswick, New Jersey, to make a supply of penicillin ready. Meanwhile, Dr. Collitti of Lutheran Hospital went off to get it. With a police escort to clear the road, Collitti made it to New Brunswick and back within two hours. Collitti gave Patricia her first dose of penicillin with just 90 minutes to spare. Six weeks later, Patricia had fully recovered and was home with her parents.

PENICILLIN SQUIBB
Sodium Salt of Penicillin
Contains 10,000 Florey units
No Preservative
KEEP BELOW 45° F.
Caution: New Drug--Limited by
federal law to investigational use

E.R. Squibb & Sons, N.Y.
Biological Laboratories,
New Brunswick, N.J.

In 1943 two-year-old Patricia Malone's life was saved when she was given the new wonder drug.

A commemorative plaque at St. Mary's Hospital, Paddington, London, records where Fleming discovered penicillin in 1928.

The first antibiotic

Patricia Malone was one of dozens of patients who were seemingly snatched from death as doctors explored just what penicillin could do. After the drug's accidental discovery in 1928 by Alexander Fleming, a Scotsman working in London, England, it had remained a mystery for ten years. Finally, two researchers at Oxford University in Oxford, England— the Australian Howard Florey and the German Ernst Chain—managed to turn it into a usable drug.

They conducted their first trial on February 12, 1941, using penicillin to treat Oxford policeman Albert Alexander. He was dangerously sick with infections caused by a simple scratch from a rose bush, but within 24 hours his condition had improved dramatically. Within a few days he was recovering strongly, but then their supply of penicillin ran out. The doctors desperately tried to recycle some of the drug from his urine. It was not enough, and Alexander died of blood poisoning on March 15. This experience showed that curing diseases with penicillin would be a matter of quantity as well as quality.

From Magic to Medicine

Western medicine began in ancient Egypt and Greece. The roots of medicine in China and India are equally old. All four systems had some ideas in common:

- Good health depends on keeping a balance of forces within the body
- Diet and climate affect health
- Many plants can heal illnesses.

Greek medical knowledge was summed up by Galen (about C.E. 129–216), whose books were still being used to train doctors in the 1600s.

Medieval doctors' treatments included drugs, baths, bleeding, and massages. They could fix simple fractures and **dislocations** and could remove stones from the bladder and cataracts from the eye. They could even do simple skin grafts, but **surgery** was usually a last resort. If the patient survived the pain, death usually followed from infection.

Knowledge of **anatomy** was limited because the church usually opposed **dissection**.

Many medieval treatments are accepted in modern science, but many others had non-scientific roots, such as **astrology**. Doctors were also powerless against **epidemics** of infectious diseases, such as influenza and smallpox. Between 1347 and 1351, the "Black Death"—bubonic plague— killed about one-third of the population of Europe.

Doctors were powerless to treat victims during London's last plague epidemic, which killed at least 80,000 people in 1665.

Pioneers of progress

Medical theory and practice improved greatly after 1500, thanks to adventurous new thinkers.

- The German Paracelsus (1493–1541) publicly burned Galen's books. He taught that diseases were caused by factors outside the patient rather than by an "imbalance" within. He also stressed that doses of medicine should be carefully measured and was the first to understand that poisons, such as arsenic or mercury, can heal if used in small amounts.

- The Belgian Vesalius (1514–64) revolutionized the study of anatomy with an accurate textbook based on careful—though illegal—dissections.

- Englishman William Harvey (1578–1657) proved that the heart pumped blood around the body, rather than ebbing and flowing like a tide, as Galen had taught.

- Dutchman Antoni van Leeuwenhoek (1632–1723) made a microscope that could magnify images up to 300 times the size of the object. He was the first to use it to observe blood cells and **bacteria** and to examine the structure of a human hair and the anatomy of insects. The microscope showed that nature was teeming with **microorganisms** far too small to be seen with the naked eye.

Paracelsus burned the books written by the ancient Greek doctor Galen. They were still being used to teach medicine in 17th-century Europe.

Defeating Smallpox

Smallpox is caused by a **virus**, a microorganism that spreads in drops of moisture from an infected person's nose or mouth. Aches and a high fever are followed by a rash of sores that fill with pus, form scabs, and leave scars. Four out of five sufferers survive, though they may be scarred and sometimes blinded. Smallpox was a global curse for centuries, until a new step forward—inoculation—began its complete elimination.

In 1717 Lady Mary Wortley Montagu described what she saw in Turkey:

The smallpox . . . is here entirely harmless by the invention of engrafting, which is the term they give it . . . old women . . . perform the operation every fall . . . the old woman comes with a nutshell full of the matter of the best sort of smallpox . . . She immediately rips open . . . and puts into the vein as much matter as can lie upon the head of her needle.

Edward Jenner MD FRS
1749-1823
Country Doctor Who Benefited Mankind

In Jenner's time, smallpox was a dreaded disease worldwide and caused many deaths particularly of children. Survivors were left badly scarred and often blinded or deformed.

In 1796 Jenner vaccinated James Phipps with cowpox and showed that the boy was then immune to smallpox. He predicted the worldwide eradication of smallpox. This was finally achieved in 1980.

Jenner was born, practised and died in Berkeley Gloucestershire and studied at St. George's Hospital, London.

This statue by William Calder Marshall RA was inaugurated by Prince Albert, the Prince Consort and was the first to be erected in Kensington Gardens in 1862. The cost was met by international subscription.

This plaque was funded and placed here by the friends of Hyde Park and Kensington Gardens, The Jenner Educational Trust and St George's Hospital Medical School in 1996, the Bicentennial Anniversary of Jenner's discovery.

Inoculation

Inoculation means giving a person a weakened form of a disease so that his or her body produces its own **antibodies** to fight the infection and become **immunized** from it in the future. Inoculation against smallpox was probably known in ancient India and China.

Inoculation, often using hawthorns instead of needles, was widely practiced in 18th-century England, after an experiment on six condemned criminals proved it was safe. Mass inoculations were performed on people judged especially at risk because they were crowded together in prisons, **poorhouses**, army barracks, or boarding schools.

Edward Jenner, who developed vaccination, is commemorated in this plaque beneath his statue in Kensington Gardens in London.

In 1802 the British Anti-Vaccination Society asked cartoonist James Gillray to predict the effects of the new treatment. His cartoon shows people who have been vaccinated turning into cows.

Vaccination

Edward Jenner (1749–1823), a country doctor from England, improved on inoculation by developing vaccination, or using a **vaccine** (from the Latin *vacca*, meaning "a cow"). Jenner was told by local people that milkmaids, who often caught cowpox from the cows they milked, never caught smallpox. In 1796 he vaccinated eight-year-old James Phipps with pus scraped from the cowpox-infected hand of milkmaid Sarah Nelmes. Six weeks later, Jenner inoculated James with full-blown smallpox, which failed to develop. James had been successfully immunized.

Jenner published a report of his experiment in 1798. It was translated into seven languages, and vaccination was soon used to fight a smallpox epidemic in far-away Kentucky. **Parliament** gave Jenner a large sum of money, and the French leader Napoleon had a medal made in his honor.

Vaccination was a real breakthrough in medicine, but it was based on **folklore** and experience, not science. A century passed before scientists understood what a virus was. In 1966 smallpox was still found in 33 countries, causing up to fifteen million cases annually and killing two million people. Finally, by 1980 the World Health Organization was able to announce that it had been completely wiped out.

9

Science Strengthens Medicine

Nineteenth-century scientists working in laboratories made many discoveries that helped doctors. At the same time, better communications allowed researchers all over the world to keep in touch, sharing ideas and information. In this way, medical science became an international matter.

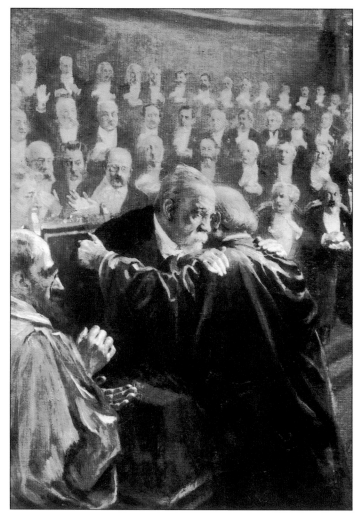

Lister embraces Pasteur at the tribute to Pasteur and his work, held at the Sorbonne in Paris to celebrate the French scientist's 70th birthday.

Pasteur

Frenchman Louis Pasteur (1822–95) was a chemist, not a doctor, whose discoveries changed medicine forever. He studied fermentation, the process by which bacteria, **molds**, and **yeasts** break down **organic** materials into simpler substances. Fermentation processes are essential in making cheese, wine, and beer. However, they can also be harmful. Pasteur discovered that controlled heating kills harmful **microbes**. This process is called pasteurization.

Pasteur's most important discovery—later known as his germ theory—was that **germs** cause diseases. Building on Jenner's work, he systematically developed vaccines against killer diseases such as anthrax and rabies. Nevertheless, many doctors were slow to recognize Pasteur's breakthrough.

Koch

German doctor Robert Koch (1843–1910) identified the **bacilli** that cause anthrax, tuberculosis, and cholera. He also experimented with dyes to stain microorganisms so that they could be identified more easily.

Semmelweis

Hungarian Ignaz Semmelweis (1818–65) believed that hospital doctors themselves spread infection. For example, **puerperal fever** killed 12 out of every 100 mothers who went into the hospital to give birth. Semmelweis insisted that washing their hands and instruments thoroughly in a **disinfectant** after examining each patient would prevent doctors from passing infection from one patient to another. At the time, Pasteur's germ theory was not generally known. Other doctors ignored Semmelweis because, although he was correct in accusing them of spreading infection, he could not show how it happened.

Pasteur's follower transforms surgery

Englishman Joseph Lister (1827–1912) quickly accepted Pasteur's germ theory. He thought it explained why almost half of all patients developed fatal infections after surgery. In 1867 Lister began soaking his surgical instruments and dressings in carbolic acid, a powerful disinfectant. This procedure, known as **antiseptic** surgery, dramatically cut the number of deaths from infection after operations. Doctors became more confident about trying trickier operations on the stomach, throat, and head, which would have previously resulted in fatal infections.

Lister, Pasteur, and Koch are honored on the front of the London School of Hygiene and Tropical Medicine.

A Life in Science

The discoveries of Pasteur and Lister resulted from experiments with patients and methodical tests. In contrast, Alexander Fleming (1881–1955) discovered penicillin by sheer chance, just as chance had made him a researcher in the first place. Born a farmer's son in Ayrshire, Scotland, Fleming grew up with an interest in plants and wildlife. At fourteen he went to London to live with his doctor half-brother, Tom, in order to learn bookkeeping. At sixteen Fleming began work as a clerk with the America Line shipping company. At eighteen he joined the London Scottish Rifle Volunteers, meeting other young Scots who were living in London and becoming a very good shot himself!

Prize-winning study ...

In 1901 an uncle of Fleming's died and left him £250—as much as a skilled workman might earn in a whole year. Now he could afford to train as a doctor, like his half-brother Tom. He went to London's newest teaching hospital, St. Mary's, Paddington. There, he became a prize-winning student but still found time for amateur acting and rifle-shooting. When Fleming qualified as a doctor in 1906, John Freeman, a researcher who wanted to keep Fleming on the hospital rifle team, suggested he work alongside him under Almroth Wright.

This shows Alexander Fleming (front row, left of aisle) as a young medical student at St. Mary's Hospital.

... and research

Fleming was given the job of taking samples of blood and saliva, then growing bacterial **cultures** in **Petri dishes** and testing them to develop vaccines. After winning the University of London Gold Medal in 1908, he qualified as a surgeon the next year. By now, though, he was a dedicated researcher and he rejected a career as a surgeon in order to continue his scientific work.

Research at war

During World War I (1914–18), Fleming served under Almroth Wright in a French military hospital, trying to reduce the number of deaths from wound infections. Fleming showed that even the strong antiseptics first used by Semmelweis and Lister failed to get into the deepest wounds. Worse still, strong antiseptics could even block the body's natural way of healing itself.

Sir Almroth Wright returned to the army during World War I. This was the first war in which soldiers were required to be vaccinated against typhoid fever.

The boss

Almroth Wright (1861–1947), the son of an Irish father and Swedish mother, became chief **pathologist** at the Army School of Medicine in England. He wanted soldiers going overseas to be vaccinated against **typhoid** fever. The army allowed soldiers to volunteer for vaccination but refused to force them. As a result, during the South African Boer War of 1899 to 1902, thousands more British soldiers died of typhoid than in battle. Wright left the army in protest, went to St. Mary's Hospital, and built up a research team. During World War I, the army finally followed Wright's advice. Once all soldiers were vaccinated, the cases of typhoid fell from 10 to 2 percent, and the proportion of those who died fell from one in seven to almost none.

Dissolving in Tears

A messy desk

After the war, Fleming was given a new laboratory at St. Mary's, but his desk remained as famously messy as ever. Other researchers cleared up daily, but Fleming left culture dishes lying around until he needed the space for new ones. Although he worked methodically, he knew scientific discoveries can be accidental. Like his hero, Pasteur, Fleming believed "chance favors the prepared mind." It was essential, therefore, to watch for anything unusual.

Alexander Fleming studies at his desk.

A killer cold

One day, when Fleming was suffering from a bad cold, he decided to culture his nasal **mucus**. The culture dish became **contaminated** by microorganisms, either from laboratory dust or blown in from outside. Two weeks later, when clearing away some Petri dishes, Fleming noticed that the one with the mucus had grown golden bacteria. They did not grow everywhere, though. The mucus itself and the surrounding area were clear and lifeless—bacteria-free, in fact. Fleming decided that something had spread out from the mucus, preventing germs from growing around it and killing off distant bacteria that had already grown.

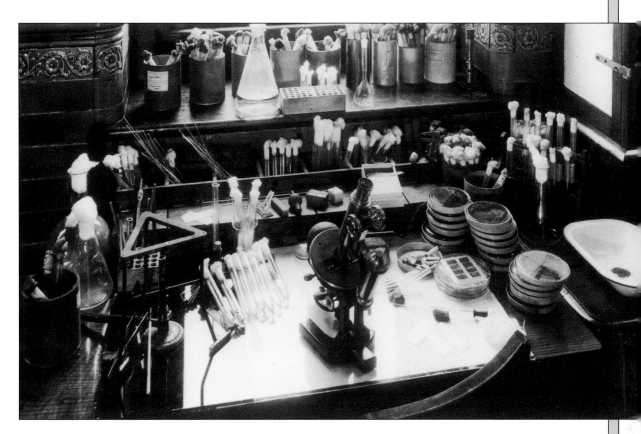

Fleming's workbench was no doubt cleaned up for this photograph!

Testing and reporting

To prove that it was not only his own nasal mucus that had the ability to kill bacteria, Fleming tested samples from other people. Then, he discovered that human tears, saliva, blood, and even pus all had bacteria-killing powers. By careful observation, Fleming had found the body's own antiseptic. He called it "lysozyme," from the Greek word *lysis*, meaning "dissolving."

Fleming lectured about lysozyme to the Medical Research Club, Unfortunately, since he was not a good public speaker, he failed to convince his audience that lysozyme was important. He still thought it was, though, partly as one of the ways the body naturally fights infection and partly because, unlike strong chemical antiseptics, lysozyme killed bacteria without damaging human cells. He later discovered that lysozyme in egg white was a hundred times stronger than in human tears. Injecting egg-white solution into rabbits made them more resistant to infection, but Fleming was not a sufficiently skilled chemist to make lysozyme powerful enough to work in humans. This was finally done at Oxford University in 1937. Since then, lysozyme has been used as a gentle antiseptic for eye infections and for preserving foodstuffs against bacterial decay.

15

Penicillin

Here, look at this...

In September 1928, Fleming was writing a chapter on the group of bacteria called staphylococci for a new textbook. It is said that one day he picked up a couple of old, moldy dishes of staphylococci colonies to show a visitor what he was doing. Looking closely at one of them, he saw to his surprise that the area around the mold was clear and bacteria-free. The rest, away from the mold, was covered in a yellow, particularly harmful bacteria.

Testing...

Fleming set out to investigate this bacteria-killing mold methodically. He put some in a separate dish, let it grow, and then watered it down. Testing this diluted form, he discovered it would still kill bacteria when it was only $1/500$ of its original strength. Fleming eventually identified the mold as one of a well-known group of brush-shaped microorganisms called *Penicillium*, from the Latin word for "a fine paintbrush." The particular type that Fleming showed to have bacteria-killing power was *Penicillium notatum*. Fleming decided to call his discovery penicillin.

This is the tower of St. Mary's Hospital, Paddington, London, in which Fleming worked.

...testing

As with lysozyme,
Fleming tried to find
where else penicillin could
be found, testing molds from
decayed food, rags, and old boots.
Meanwhile, the original penicillin was tested for harmful side effects
on mice, rabbits, and a human volunteer—Fleming's assistant, Stuart
Craddock. Fleming was relieved to find none. Unfortunately, it proved
difficult to keep penicillin active long enough to try it out as a treatment
for actual patients. Its bacteria-killing powers faded after a few days, and
Fleming was not a good enough chemist to stabilize it.

Reporting

Fleming took his research into penicillin as far as he could. In the June
1929 issue of the *British Journal of Experimental Pathology*, he
published an account of it, the first-ever detailed report of an **antibiotic**.
Fleming's lecture on penicillin to the Medical Research Club roused as
little interest as his earlier talk on lysozyme had done. For years nothing
further was done with penicillin. Fleming himself turned to testing a new
family of drugs, sulfonamides, for which great claims were made. His tests
showed that they stopped bacteria from spreading but could not kill
them off. Patients were still ultimately cured by their own bodies' natural
defenses. Meanwhile, the possibilities of penicillin were all but forgotten.

A Breakthrough

Brains from abroad

A **Rhodes Scholarship** brought Australian scientist Howard Florey (1898–1968) to research at Oxford University in 1922. By 1935 he was a professor. As an editor of the *British Journal of Experimental Pathology*, Florey knew of Fleming's work almost from its beginnings. Needing a chemist assistant, he asked Ernst Chain (1906–1979), a Jewish refugee from Nazi Germany, to join him in Oxford to research just how lysozyme acted chemically to kill bacteria.

Penicillin again

As part of the preparation for his research, Chain read Fleming's 1929 article about penicillin. He became interested in the problem of making it in batches large enough, pure enough, and active for long enough to be used as a treatment. With Florey's encouragement and the brilliant technical assistance of Norman Heatley, an English researcher, Chain finally succeeded where everyone else had failed. In fact, it was later shown that the penicillin they produced was still only 2 percent pure! Fermentation is a complicated process and not easy to control precisely.

Australian scientist Howard Florey was awarded the Albert Gold Medal jointly with Alexander Fleming in 1946 for his part in research on penicillin.

More testing

With good supplies of penicillin, it became possible to run extensive tests. One involved injecting 50 mice with streptococci bacteria. Half were then injected with penicillin. After 16 hours, 24 of the 25 that had received penicillin were still alive and all the rest were dead. Further tests confirmed Fleming's findings of ten years before—that penicillin was both a dramatically powerful killer of bacteria and quite harmless to animals and humans.

With Florey's encouragement and Heatley's help, biochemist Ernest Chain (below) solved the problem of producing batches of penicillin that were sufficiently large and pure for effective treatment.

Publishing

In August 1940—a year after the outbreak of World War II (1939–45)—Florey, Chain, and Heatley published an account of their research in *The Lancet*, Britain's leading medical journal. Their article, *Penicillin as a Chemotherapeutic Agent*, paid full tribute to Fleming's pioneering work. However, the authors clearly believed that he had died because they referred to him as "the late Professor Fleming." Still very much alive, Fleming immediately went to Oxford, announced himself as "the late Fleming," and asked "'to see what you've been doing with my old penicillin," but he took no part in the Oxford team's further researches. Fleming returned to St. Mary's to tend to patients wounded during the bombing of London.

A Problem of Production

Human trials

Between February and June 1941, the Oxford team used penicillin to treat six desperately sick patients with no other hope of recovery; four survived. It seemed penicillin might save thousands of soldiers from dying of infected wounds, but Oxford could only produce it in quantities large enough for laboratory tests or for treating individual patients—not for whole armies.

The manager of a New York drugstore is shown putting up a sign for the new wonder drug, penicillin, in March 1945.

Help in Illinois

Although the United Kingdom had survived the threat of invasion in 1940, its situation was still desperate. Soldiers wounded in battle and civilians wounded in bombings could all benefit from penicillin, but British drug companies lacked the funds to develop large-scale production.

The United States, however, was rich and not yet at war. Florey and Heatley traveled there in July 1941. An old friend of Florey's, Charles Thom, from the U.S. Department of Agriculture, put them in touch with the Northern Regional Research Laboratory in Peoria, Illinois. They asked local people to bring them examples of moldy food in case one example might yield an even better source of penicillin. One did so: a moldy melon from a Peoria market. It yielded a chemically stable strain of penicillin ideal for medical use. Thanks to this chance discovery, the Peoria team was able to produce penicillin eight times stronger than the Oxford variety.

The U.S. joins in

Japan's attack on Pearl Harbor in December 1941 brought the United States into the war. Giant U.S. drug companies teamed up with the government to mass produce medicines for the war effort. Top priority, however, was given to measures to protect troops fighting in tropical areas against bites from poisonous insects and **malaria**, which is carried by mosquitoes. Meanwhile, back in the UK, Florey's wife, Ethel, who was a doctor, was testing penicillin on some of her patients. Their complaints ranged from abscesses and infected wounds to a baby whose spine was severely twisted by osteomyelitis, a bone infection.

A U.S. laboratory technician prepares penicillin in 1945.

A wonder drug

By September 1942, penicillin had been used to treat 187 different conditions. Sometimes it was given as an injection, sometimes it was used as an ointment, and sometimes it was swallowed as a medicine—but almost always with success. Fleming himself used it to cure a family friend of meningitis, an infection of the brain or spinal cord that can be fatal. This was another dramatic first. This led Fleming to contact friends in government. A Penicillin Committee was soon established to get British drug companies to begin mass production.

Into Battle

Trial by disaster

On November 29, 1942, a fire at Boston's Coconut Grove nightclub caused a stampede, killing nearly 500 and injuring about 200. Many suffered terrible burns that could easily become infected. Dr. Chester Keefer, in charge of U.S. penicillin production, ordered supplies to be released to Massachusetts General Hospital in Boston. News leaked out that the Merck drug company in Rahway, New Jersey, had worked around the clock to rush out a batch of "an unnamed miracle drug."

Keefer was encouraged by the Coconut Grove cases to begin testing penicillin on wounded soldiers in spring 1943. Provided the penicillin was given in large enough doses, even heavily infected wounds could be cured. These tests convinced the U.S. Army to push penicillin production as the drug companies' top priority.

A U.S. poster shows how penicillin caught the imagination of the public.

Tested in action ...

The first large supply of penicillin was delivered to the United Kingdom in May 1943, and it was used under Florey's direction in North Africa in June. Experience there showed it was best used as soon as possible after a wound had been sustained, rather than waiting for the casualty to be evacuated to a safe area.

...with dramatic results

Sufficient penicillin was soon available in the UK to treat victims of factory accidents as well as battle casualties. By D-Day, on June 6, 1944, when the Allies landed in France, Ethel Florey was in charge of a special penicillin unit treating 3,000 casualties from the Normandy landings. During World War I, over 12 percent of wounded soldiers treated in frontline hospitals died of infections. In contrast, by 1944 this number was almost zero. By 1945 the United States was producing enough penicillin to provide 34 million doses a day.

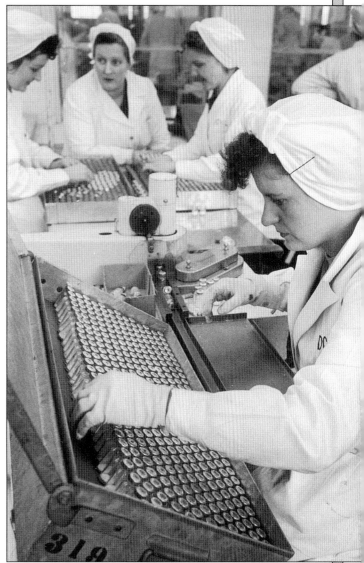

This shows large-scale penicillin production at the Speke factory in Liverpool, England, in 1954.

A soldier's thanks

As a surgeon at Massachusetts General Hospital, Champ Lyons had used penicillin to treat burns cases from the Coconut Grove fire. As a U.S. Army major treating U.S. soldiers (GIs) wounded in Italy, Lyons received the following letter from a soldier with a shattered thigh. The soldier clearly realized that he owed his life to penicillin as well as to the surgeon's skilled care:

"You will not remember me, I was just another scared GI patient to you. But I will surely remember you, always. You ... operated on me ...in Naples. ... I shall never forget those penicillin shots (injections), one every four hours ...for what seemed an eternity."

Because the needles had to be large to allow the penicillin to pass into the body, the injections were painful—but they worked.

Prizewinners

Sir Alexander

As penicillin came into general use, the public saw what a massive breakthrough it was in saving lives. It became clear that the people who made it possible should be honored by more than just other scientists. A month after the Allied landings in France, British King George VI knighted both Fleming, as the discoverer of penicillin, and Florey, as leader of the team that had turned it into a usable treatment. Knighthood is a high honor given by the British king or queen to recognize achievement.

A year later, in 1945, Fleming and Florey, this time with Chain, met another king, in Stockholm, where the Swedish monarch presented them with the Nobel Prize for Medicine (see page 25).

Celebrity

Howard Florey and Ernst Chain had no wish to become celebrities and returned to their research work. In 1960 Florey was elected to the most honored position in British science—president of the Royal Society—and was the first Australian to hold the post. Chain directed an international research center in Rome and was finally knighted in 1969.

This is Fleming's Nobel Prize medal.

It was left to Fleming to become the center of public attention. His career as a researcher was over and he had time to enjoy his fame. He also valued the chance to speak out for science in general. He was careful not to exaggerate what he had done, paying tribute to Florey's team and modestly saying, "Nature makes penicillin; I just found it."

A global hero

Fleming received honors throughout his native England. He was also honored in France, in Spain, and by the pope. In the United States, the Kiowa tribe made him an honorary chief. In dozens of towns and cities, streets and squares were named after him. Fleming died in 1955 and was buried in London's St. Paul's Cathedral, beside Britain's greatest heroes.

A stained-glass window honors Fleming in St. James's, Sussex Gardens, a few minutes' walk from St. Mary's Hospital, London, where he worked.

The Nobel Prize

Alfred Nobel (1833–96), the Swedish inventor of dynamite, left a fortune to fund prizes for outstanding achievements in chemistry, physics, medicine, literature, and peace. Prizes were first awarded in 1901. Prizewinners for medicine include Sir Ronald Ross, who discovered how to fight malaria, and Sir Frederick Banting, the Canadian discoverer of insulin, which is used to treat diabetes.

Battling On

Swallow this

After World War II, there was time and money to develop better types of penicillin. One variety, penicillin V, proved chemically stable when mixed with the natural acid in the patient's stomach. It could therefore be swallowed rather than injected, making it faster, cheaper, and less painful to give to patients. Penicillin V became the family doctor's first-choice antibiotic.

Evolution: Fast forward

Bacteria have been around for over three billion years. Since they can reproduce themselves every 30 minutes or so, they evolve much faster than human beings. It was not surprising then that some bacteria developed resistance to penicillin, which was noticed by Florey as early as 1940. By 1946 London hospitals recorded that 15 percent of infections from the bacteria *Staphylococcus aureus* were resistant to penicillin G, the standard form at the time. By 1947 the figure was 40 percent, and by 1948 it was 60 percent. Researchers raced to develop new penicillins to combat resistant bacteria.

Penicillium notatum, Fleming's original source of penicillin, is shown magnified many times through a microscope.

Another step forward

Penicillin did not work against typhoid or **salmonella**, and some patients were fatally allergic to it. In 1945, in the Italian island of Sardinia, researcher Giuseppe Brotzu identified a mold growing on sewage that could kill typhoid bacilli. In 1961 Florey's team produced cephalosporin, which is suitable for patients allergic to penicillin and is effective against throat infections, typhoid, **pneumonia**, and **diphtheria**.

The white plague

The success of penicillin inspired research. Scientists and doctors began testing other molds in the search for substances that would kill microbes unaffected by penicillin.

Ordinary soil proved to be a profitable source of molds. One yielded a cure for tuberculosis (TB), which has probably caused more premature deaths than any other disease in history. One-third of the world's population carries the bacillus that causes TB, but people only develop the disease if they are not healthy enough to fight off infection. TB still kills three million people a year, mostly in overcrowded cities in poor countries.

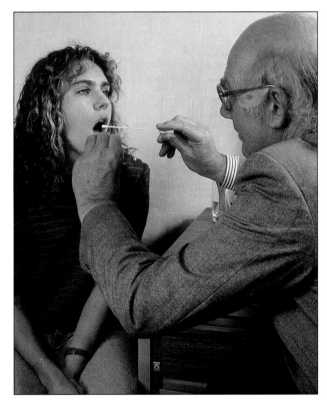

Some patients seem to think that doctors can produce a wonder drug to cure any illness.

French researchers Albert Calmette and Camille Guérin had produced a TB vaccine in 1924. In 1943 the U.S. doctor Selman A. Waksman, an expert on soil microorganisms, discovered streptomycin— the first drug effective against TB. Waksman won the 1952 Nobel Prize for Medicine for this discovery. Since streptomycin can sometimes cause dizziness, deafness, and kidney damage, it has since been replaced by other drugs. By the 21st century, TB was once again on the increase, so the search for better treatments continues.

The Great Debate

Luck or judgement?

Sir Alexander Fleming is hailed as one of the world's greatest scientists. While no one would doubt that he was a very able man, does he really deserve his special reputation?

Question 1: Does Fleming deserve his reputation?

Yes!

- Fleming did actually discover and name penicillin.
- He had the genius to interpret what others had seen but failed to appreciate (the antibiotic properties of molds).
- He devoted himself to scientific research, when he could have enjoyed a more prosperous career as a surgeon.
- Fleming made other important discoveries, apart from penicillin.

No!

- There was little point in discovering penicillin if the research on how it worked and how to use it was not completed. Fleming failed to isolate the active ingredient in his "penicillin" substance.
- If it had not been for Florey and Chain, Fleming's work might have been useless.
- Fleming failed in one of the key elements of medical research: making the results of his work widely known so that they could benefit others.
- Fleming's discovery owed more to luck (and even his bad practice by leaving dishes uncleaned) than judgment.

What do you think?

Bacteria such as MRSA, pictured here, are developing resistance to antibiotics. What will we do about them in the future?

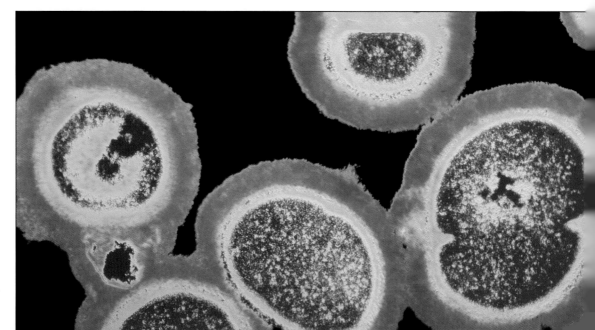

Miracle cure?

When penicillin and other antibiotics first appeared, it was popularly believed that they were the cure for just about everything, from the common cold to cancer. Were they really as wonderful as people believed?

Question 2: Has the impact of antibiotics been exaggerated?

Yes!

- Partly because of widespread over-prescription, strains of bacteria swiftly developed immunity to many forms of antibiotic, making antibiotic treatment ineffective.
- Once bacterial infections could normally be cured easily, doctors and nurses paid less attention to cleanliness; this made hospitals more dangerous and fuelled the spread of so-called superbugs, such as MRSA.
- The widespread use of antibiotics in animal feeds, such as for chicken and cattle, led to even more strains of bacteria becoming resistant to antibiotics.
- Antibiotics have no effect on many deadly diseases caused by viruses, such as HIV and AIDS, flu, and even colds.

No!

Antibiotics had a huge impact when they were first introduced, saving countless numbers of people from death by bacterial infection.

- Surgery has become much safer with the advent of antibiotics, allowing more complicated, life-saving operations.
- Antibiotics have helped farmers by keeping their animals in good health.
- Killer diseases, such as TB and typhoid, have been all but eliminated in many parts of the world through the use of antibiotics.

What do you think?

Find Out More

Using the Internet

Explore the Internet to find out more about the discovery of penicillin. You can use a search engine, such as www.yahooligans.com or www.google.com, and type in keywords such as *Fleming*, *smallpox*, *Pasteur*, *vaccinations*, or *inoculation*.

More Books to Read

Gogerly, Liz. *Scientists Who Made History: Louis Pasteur*. Chicago: Raintree, 2002.

Morgan, Sally. *Science at the Edge: Fighting Disease*.
    Chicago: Heinemann Library, 2002.

Townsend, John. *A Painful History of Medicine: Pox, Pus and Plagues*.
    Chicago: Raintree, 2006.

Timeline

1717	Lady Montagu observes inoculation in Turkey
1796	Edward Jenner experiments successfully with vaccination against smallpox
1822	Birth of Louis Pasteur
1867	Joseph Lister pioneers the use of antiseptics in surgery
1881	Birth of Alexander Fleming
1888	Pasteur Institute for Research founded in Paris
1898	Birth of Australian Howard Florey
1914–18	World War I
1922	Fleming discovers lysozyme
1924	Calmette and Guérin develop an anti-tuberculosis vaccine
1928	Fleming discovers penicillin
1935	Florey invites Chain to join his research team at Oxford
1939–45	World War II
1940	Florey, Chain, and Heatley publish the results of their laboratory tests on penicillin
1941	Penicillin first used to treat human patients
1942	Fleming uses penicillin to cure a case of meningitis
1943	Selman Waksman discovers streptomycin
1944	June 6: D-Day—Allies invade Normandy to begin the liberation of France
	Florey and Fleming are knighted
1945	Fleming, Florey, and Chain share Nobel Prize for Medicine
1952	Selman Waksman wins Nobel Prize for Medicine
1955	Death of Sir Alexander Fleming
1960	Florey is elected president of the Royal Society
1961	Florey's team isolates cephalosporin
1980	World Health Organization (WHO) announces that smallpox has been wiped out worldwide
1987	Azidothymidine (AZT) introduced to combat HIV
1993	WHO declares a global emergency over reemergence of tuberculosis; there are three million deaths per year
1994	French scientists manufacture Taxol, an anti-cancer drug, from yew-tree needles
2006	Deaths due to MRSA, an antibiotic-resistant "superbug," continue to rise in hospitals. Drug companies race to find a cure.

Glossary

anatomy study of the structure of the body

antibiotic substance that kills bacteria, especially those that cause illness

antibody natural defense substance produced by the body

antiseptic chemical that kills bacteria, especially those that cause disease or rotting

astrology belief that events can be predicted by the movements of stars and planets

bacillus bacteria shaped like a rod, such as staphylococci

bacteria tiny one-celled life-forms visible only through a microscope; some are harmless, others cause rotting or disease

contaminate mix in something that makes a substance less pure

culture bacteria grown experimentally for study

diphtheria highly infectious disease of the throat, often fatal in children

disinfectant chemical that kills bacteria that cause infections

dislocation displaced bone

dissection cutting up dead bodies to study them

epidemic widespread outbreak of disease

folklore popular or traditional beliefs, often based on experience

germ popular name for a microorganism that causes disease

immunize protect against a disease by giving someone a very mild form of it

infection disease spread by microorganisms getting into the body

malaria infectious disease spread by mosquitoes; sufferers are severely weakened by alternate chills and bouts of fever

microbe/ microorganism any organism, such as bacteria, viruses, molds, or yeasts, too small to be seen without a microscope

mold fungus that develops on organic materials such as food, leather, and cloth

mucus slimy substance that protects sensitive skin inside the nose, for example

organic something that is living or has lived

parliament group responsible for making laws in some countries

pathologist expert on the causes of disease and death

Petri dish shallow glass container used in a laboratory to grow cultures

pneumonia infection that causes the lungs to fill with liquid, which causes death when the patient can no longer breathe

poorhouse hostel where people too poor to keep themselves were fed and sheltered, often in harsh conditions

puerperal fever form of blood poisoning caused by infection caught during childbirth

Rhodes Scholarship award funded by money given by diamond millionaire Cecil Rhodes (1853–1902) to enable outstanding students from the United States and other countries to study at Oxford University, in England

salmonella type of bacteria, many varieties of which cause food poisoning

surgery cutting into the body to repair damage or remove infection

typhoid highly infectious and often fatal fever caused by a bacillus

vaccine substance used to immunize against a particular disease

virus microorganism that can only reproduce within the cells of something living

yeast single-celled form of fungus

Index

AIDS 29, 30
Alexander, Albert 5
anatomy 6, 7
anthrax 10
antibiotics 17, 26, 27, 28–29
    over-use of 28, 29
antibodies 8
antiseptics 11, 13, 15, 30
azidothymidine (AZT) 30

bacilli 27
bacteria 7, 10, 14, 15, 16,
    17, 18, 26, 29
    resistant bacteria 26, 29
bacterial decay 15
Banting, Frederick 25
battle casualties 22, 23
Black Death 6
Brotzu, Giuseppe 27

Calmette, Albert 27, 30
cephalosporin 27, 30
Chain, Ernst 5, 18, 19, 24, 30
cholera 10
Craddock, Stuart 17
cultures 13, 14

diphtheria 27
disinfectants 11

epidemics 6, 9

fermentation 10, 18
Fleming, Sir Alexander 5,
    12–17, 19, 21, 24, 25,
    28, 30
Florey, Ethel 21, 23
Florey, Howard 5, 18, 19,
    20, 24, 26, 30
Freeman, John 12

Galen 6, 7
germ theory of disease 10,
    11
Greek medical theory and
    practice 6
Guérin, Camille 27, 30

Harvey, William 7
Heatley, Norman 18, 19, 20,
    30
HIV 28, 29

immunization 8, 9
infections 4, 5, 6, 8, 11, 13,
    15, 22, 23, 26, 27
influenza 6, 29
inoculation 8, 9
insulin 25

Jenner, Edward 8, 9, 10, 30

Keefer, Chester 4, 22
Koch, Robert 10, 11

Leeuwenhoek, Antoni van 7
Lister, Joseph 11, 13, 30
Lyons, Champ 23
lysozyme 15, 18, 30

malaria 21, 25
Malone, Patricia 4, 5
medical theory and practice
    in history 6–11
medieval theory and practice
    6
meningitis 21, 30
microbes/microorganisms 7,
    8, 10, 14, 16, 27
molds 10, 16, 17, 20, 27
Montagu, Lady Mary
    Wortley 8, 30
mucus 14

Nobel, Alfred 25
Nobel Prize for Medicine 24,
    25, 27, 30

Paracelsus 7
Pasteur, Louis 10, 11, 14, 30
pasteurization 10
penicillin 4–5, 16–17, 18, 19,
    20, 21–23, 24, 26–27,
    28, 29, 30
    allergic reactions 27

discovery of 5, 12,
    16–17, 30
    human trials 20, 21, 30
    penicillin G 26
    penicillin V 26
    production 18, 20, 21,
    22, 23
    resistance to 26
plagues 6, 27
pneumonia 27
puerperal fever 11

rabies 10
Ross, Sir Ronald 25

St. Mary's Hospital,
    Paddington 5, 12, 13,
    14, 16
salmonella 27
Semmelweis, Ignaz 11, 13
smallpox 6, 8, 9, 30
spread of diseases 29
staphylococci bacteria 16, 26
streptococci bacteria 19
streptomycin 27, 30
sulfonamides 17
surgery 6, 11

Taxol 30
throat infections 27
tuberculosis (TB) 10, 27, 30
typhoid fever 13, 27

vaccination 9, 10, 13
Vesalius 7
viruses 8, 9, 29

Waksman, Selman A. 27, 30
wonder drugs 27
World War I 13
World War II 19, 20, 21,
    22–23
Wright, Sir Almroth 12, 13

yeasts 10